SOUL BE A WITNESS
Songs to Boys of Color

John Warner Smith

MadHat Press
Asheville, North Carolina

MadHat Press
MadHat Incorporated
PO Box 8364, Asheville, NC 28814

The Library of Congress has assigned
this edition a Control Number of
2015957714

ISBN 978-1-941196-26-7 (paperback)

Text by John Warner Smith
Cover illustration by Dennis Paul Williams
Photography by Philip Gould
Cover design by Marc Vincenz

www.MadHat-Press.com

First Printing

SOUL BE A WITNESS

SONGS TO BOYS OF COLOR

Acknowledgments

Grateful acknowledgment is made to the editors and readers of the following journals where poems in this collection have appeared:

About Place Journal:	"Bucket"
	"Fences"
Antioch Review:	"Baptism"
Fjords Review:	"Parted"
Kestrel:	"An Artist Reflects on His Creations"
MockingHeart Review:	"Baby and the Bell Ringers"
	"Spirit"
Pembroke Magazine:	"Rebirth"
Pluck!:	"After Conner, Wallace, Helms, and Duke"
Quiddity:	"Mrs. Taylor's Lunch Table"
River Styx:	"The Shaving Mirror"
Transition:	"Dumb"
	"Hands"
	"Higher Ground"
	"A Letter from John D."
	"Reply to the Letter from John D."
Tupelo Quarterly:	"Stars"

Table of Contents

For Patrick

NATIVE SON

DUMB

after Warsan Shire

Your son is dumb, a nobody,
without honor, country or history.
Talk to him.
The books he reads do not.

Have you not told him
life is mean but fair,
God created the stars, wind and sea
and slave ships passed,
God parted the sea
and slave masters drowned?

So what, that your son's belly
bears the marks of your teeth
and blunt edges of your fist.
So what, that his father is a ravaging wolf.
Your son is a shark
with no reverence for life,
not even his own.
Does he not know
that no loving outstretched arms,
no prayer, salt or grail will save him?

Fathers tell their daughters
to not go near him,
not let his words be pomegranates
or the soft-drip thaw of ice on the myrtles.
They tell their daughters
your son grows like a reed in the wind
and dreams only when he sleeps.
Talk to your son.

John Warner Smith

Tell him what it means to be a man.

Why the blindfolding fog
between his hand on a trigger
and the barb-wired walls
that will bend his knees?
Why the gorge
between his head and heart?
Can you not fill *that* hole in him?

Have you not told him
how *he* could sail the ship
that bounds and carries him,
and he needs no stars, moon or lighthouse
for the rogue waves
and swirling forked strait?
Does he not know
he can bend rivers, storm the palisade
and take back his soul?

HANDS

for my grandsons

I.

No one might ever say what I am about to tell you.
When strong men die, you don't bring up their dark pasts.
So years ago, when I eulogized your Great-Great Paw Paw André,
I didn't say that he had spent eighteen months in prison
for killing a man. The year was 1939. He was 27 with a wife
and three baby girls. The oldest, your Great-Granny Mary,
was three years old. It was Saturday night, a poker game,
the backroom of a gambling shack in Broussard.
Suddenly, an argument, a fistfight, a wooden bench slung
at André's head. The blade he pulled, smaller than his hand,
quicker than his thought, sank into a man's heart
as if André had played magic to make the knife disappear.
Named for African slaves, bound on three sides
by the murky Mississippi River, Angola Penitentiary
had been cut out of cane and corn fields of South Louisiana
plantations. The scorching sun bent iron and melted
men's spines. Shovels and sledgehammers of the farm
and quarry pulled flesh from men's hands. A good meal
was raw potatoes, bread, and water. A good night was one lived.

II.

As a young man, I had close encounters with death
and imprisonment: blue lights flashing, the life ahead of me
unreeling, told to step away from a car, show my hands,
a cop's finger pointed at my face, his hand on a holster.
One frigid Saturday morning just short of my turning 19,
Cousin Donald and I on a Harley, daredevils tunneling
wind drafts of the wheelers, got pulled over by a trooper
onto a lonely gravel road at the mouth of a cane field.

He said *you boys* but we heard "niggers." *Slam the door*
on his leg, Donald said, *and I'll reach in and grab his pistol.*
Scared but angry, I looked down at the trooper seated
behind the wheel, pen and ticket book in his hand,
driver's door open, his foot on the ground. I felt a hand
leave my body, and for more than a second I reached
for the door. Something, I don't know what, pulled me back.
So when I say that any goodness in you and me is penance,
I mean that the life we think is ours is not. Strong men cry
us into existence, and prayers of good women are answered.

BUCKET

Sometimes, when I'm the only black man in the room,
sitting under the soft, quiet glow of enlightenment,
talking about building an education system
to save mostly black children,
I feel what I felt one day in ninth grade
when I stood in a lunch line
and a slimy blob of spit hit the back of my neck
like a large, stinging rock,
and I turned around
to find a sea of white faces sneering back.

I feel what I felt years later
when a corporate recruiter said,
You're the type we'd like to groom,
and I stepped out of the city's tallest building,
wearing my blue pinstripe polyester suit,
carrying my vinyl attaché case, looking back
at a glass tower with carpet so plush
I'd kick my shoes off and think
I had arrived, until the day
my supervisor used the "n" word
when he saw a white cop beating
an old black man on a downtown street,
and I remembered a joke he told
weeks before: that when cops in Beaumont
arrested a drunk, vagrant black man
in the middle of the night
they sobered him up
by driving him ten miles
and dropping him off
at a curbside in Vidor,
where everybody was the Klan.

I feel what I felt and what my daddy
and every black man before us felt
at some time in our lives,
when a white man had something we needed
and we couldn't get it
without stooping low, bending over
and casting down a bucket,
or just keeping our mouths shut.

Stars

New Orleans, a Tuesday, 7:30 AM,
I'm sipping coffee at a McDonald's on Canal
when two young black men, early twenties perhaps,
walk in, buying nothing. Suddenly,
I'm aboard a mothership,
streaking toward the farthest stars.

One, like a fly, bobs the aisles, sweaty
in his *Crown Royal* muscle shirt.
Gym shorts hanging off his ass,
headset in his ears, he pantomimes
a singer and dances a Mardi Gras mambo
in July, with himself, second-lining
silky-smoothly across the floor, out the door,
onto the parking lot—his own block party
without the block.

The other, well-groomed, small backpack,
talks loudly, eloquently to himself
about home, what it is, isn't and should be; then,
facing the faces, he launches a soliloquy
of senseless babble,
and you sense the other—
the voices, a stage, curtain and cast,
his fans and followers looking on,
inside his head.

I'm gazing at stars. Drawn to the glow
of their wayward worlds,
I can't help
but pause, watch and listen.
I'm entertained,

9

but scared, because they're black men
and I'm one, too,
with a son and grandsons of my own,
and I can't help
but ponder: what's loose,
what's broken, what's gone wrong,
what's the fix?

BLACK BOY

after Langston Hughes

Nation Time, 1966.
Courtroom gavels slammed
like sledgehammers,
shattering glass clouds.
Quietly in the night,
a key turned and clicked,
ring-bolts snapped, and a door
wide as the Middle Passage
swung open. Standing
at the threshold,
he faced two worlds,
and stepped into the one unknown.
    I am the darker brother, he said.
    your schoolhouse Negro,
    standing for freedom.
    Make me ugly.
    Make me hurt.
    Make me cry.
He chose white teachers,
white history,
white lies,
white spit.
He chose snakes,
wolves and pious holy rollers.
    Shame me, he said.
    Make me somebody
    nobody wants
    to stand around.
    Make me your social problem.
    Make me feel lost, branded
    and hide whipped.

11

Make me ugly.
Make me hurt.
Make me cry.
He chose Tar Baby,
Monkey, Stink Bug, Sambo, Tom:
      names they called him
      when he stood in his broken shoes,
      smothering in his hopes and dreams.
But, damn, look at him standing now.

DREAM AMERICA

after Countee Cullen & Amiri Baraka

See the great line of warriors,
martyrs of protest
who dared to fight
for freedom.
Medgar, Malcolm and Martin,
trinity of sacrifice,
slain in seasons dawning,
same blood,
shed in the struggle
to be treated like humans
in the century of the bombing
of the 16th Street Baptist Church,
one hundred years after Lincoln's decree.

Men warriors, women warriors,
fathers and mothers bred for sale,
babies fed for slaughter.
See them hunted and trapped
like beasts, shackled
at the gate of no return,
at the gallows,
at the mouths of dogs and fire hoses.
See the greed and wretched waves
that wrenched them,
churched their guts and hopes
inside out.

Scattered grain, shattered legacy,
hurry, sweet child, come see
the procession of genius and strength
marching toward truth,

days and nights of terror and torment,
crosses on their flesh-torn backs.

Hear the words
they were dared to think,
dared to speak,
dared to read and write,
when told to never cry too long,
never stand too tall and straight,
never stare, never beat a drum,
never lift their heads high
and dream of being free.

See the fake politicians,
preachers and teachers
who pretend to care
and portend *your* demise.
See the dumbness they label you to be.
Hear what they say
about your heritage,
about your future,
about who and what
you think you can be and do.
Hear what they say
about your momma and daddy,
your streets, houses and schools,
your songs, stories and poems,
your mind, heart and soul.

In America, no justice, no you,
no government, no you,
no education, no you,

more guns, more drugs,
more prisons, no you,
in America.

Come child.
Dream freedom.
Dream broken antebellum clocks
and quilted fields of salt.
Dream praises
for heart flowers
and motley, opalescent skies.

Leave this crystal-palace maze.
Scale the mountain
a skyward rainbow crowns.
Sweet voices lifted, singing,
turn your eyes to the martyrs' gate,
see their molten breasts of iron,
like violets blooming on the tombs,
sprinkling tears their unborns weep.

Dream *America*.
Dream *you*.

John Warner Smith

BLACKBIRDS DON'T FLY

America 1921, Lenox Avenue.
The 369th Infantry Band swings.
Trombones and tambourines syncopate
to the tom-tom. Colored soldiers
wearing purple hearts,
decked in olive drab and crown-creased hats,
step a be-bop cadence in calypso riff:
Billy don't bend like those trees.
Billy don't run like that river.
Off your knees. Kiss some ass.
Make love if you please.
White Camellias mix kerosene cocktails.
Hoodwink, Fire Spear, and Noose,
so-called nightriders, hide
behind bed sheets, and masquerade
in mirror-less mornings.
On a twine line,
fifty-one neck bones hang.
Blackbirds don't fly.

AFTER CONNOR, WALLACE, HELMS, AND DUKE

Why the petal-soft gloves
and sweet olive curtsy,

our timidity, today,
to peel back the sharkskin

of hollow, wooden men:
broken beams of light

and chameleon shadows
seeping opaque blinds,

coloring the bitterness
they brush and bury

inside polished mirrors,
Machiavelli enlarging,

even as they pray
words too ancient, bare

and redeeming to mute
the hate they make?

FATHER

A Letter from John D.

This is something I haven't done in many years,
write a letter. I guess you can see by my penmanship
I never was much good at writing. This one is long overdue.
It was very rewarding to get to talk to you
after all these years. You are a very fine young man.
Any man should be proud to call you his son.
Your mother and her husband did one fine job
of rearing you. I can only claim the biological part.

I regret not being able to have been there
when you needed someone to lean and depend on
when you were growing up. That may have been my loss
as well as yours. Sometimes foolish pride
can cause you to cut off your nose to spite your face.
All I am sure of now is that I want to know you better,
to meet my grandchildren and their mother.

I hope God grants me enough life to try and make up
for some of my mistakes. One thing you may not know
is that I have kept abreast of your progress
and I am very proud that we wear the same first
and last name. I hope you overlook all these mistakes.
I am a little out of practice. Take care of yourself
and in between your busy schedule let me hear from you.

I remain your father,
John D.

REPLY TO THE LETTER FROM JOHN D.

One night, nearly two decades before you wrote,
I drove a few miles from home and called you

from a roadside pay phone, needing help
for my college tuition. My memory has grown

kinder over the years but in plain truth you said
no. Slowly, the sound grew faint then silent

but the wound of your words never healed.
That was the first and last time I asked

anything of you. And then, one day I heard
that my grandmother, your mother, had died.

She had always made me feel loved, like one
of her children. I learned of her death

incidentally, a week after she had been buried.
It has taken me twenty-five years to reply

to your letter. My hurt buried you long before
we laid you inside those narrow, tunneled

walls. There can be no reconciliation,
only your loss and regret, but I forgive you.

A GIFT

(Opened at Charlotte Douglas International Airport
en route to a Cave Canem Retreat)

As sons, we come into the world watching our dads
develop into fathers. We see the transitions of manhood:
the maturity from mistakes, the perfections and flaws,
always processing with a keen eye and trying
to understand what this man's role is in our lives.
Yet, we never once take into account that this
god-like figure we have created is indeed just a man.

Later, when we become men, we realize the difficulty
of living up to the expectations of others:
a black man in America with a sense of purpose
and vision for his life, the vision he has for his family,
the expectations of his peers, wife and children.
In the middle of it all, God is tugging, and you hope
that you do what's right to witness His vision for you.

As sons, we sit back and watch it all transpire:
a childhood filled with confusion, fear and anxiety,
mixed with admiration and appreciation. Growing up,
Mama challenged you to be a perfect husband.
My sisters challenged you to be a father figure.
I didn't challenge you to be a perfect father to me,
but I do recall moments when I felt elements missing,
when I felt hurt, and felt that you weren't taking time
to get to know me or to help me figure out
what it meant to be a young man. At times, I felt
that you weren't interested in having a family at all.
I knew you loved us, because you continued
to make sacrifices, but that was simply you being "Dad."

Still, through my tears and smiles, you remained
constant, teaching responsibility and discipline.

Being a husband and a father has opened my eyes
to a whole new world of manhood that, as a son,
I had no understanding of. As sons, we don't know
what it means to be a good husband or a good father.
After all these years, I still want you to be perfect.
I still want you to care, love, provide, protect, teach,
and accept me as a son. Even as a man, I am still
a runny nose kid fighting back tears to figure out
the next thing I can do to make my dad proud.

A man sees his father differently than a child sees
his dad. There is a greater appreciation for sacrifice.
There is a greater understanding of age and maturity.
A son sees his dad as someone who is a constant,
but a man understands that manhood is a transition.

Over the years, observing your transitions has been
the foundation for my perceptions of what manhood
and being a father means. For that I thank God for you,
because your transitions and my perceptions
were God at work. I gain the perception of a son
wanting his dad to be perfect, but I also get to witness
my dad become more of a man. I take pride in that
in the same way that I hope that you could
take pride in me as a son.

Happy Father's Day, Pop! I love you.
Patrick

THE SHAVING MIRROR

I arrive late with the intent of leaving early.
You have eaten dinner, and your body knows
the hour has passed for you to be strapped to a pulley,
hoisted from your chair and laid to bed until morning.
But I find pleasure in holding your face
in my hand, a son's indulgence—
to put sweetened bread within your reach
like a teething toy, then lean over
your drooping torso and groom you,
tugging at your stiffened neck,
your fingers grabbing and pinching like claws.

Your face in my hand—
once child's play, now darkened, tarnished glass.
Shaving your gray, stubborn stubbles, I hum
a tuneless song to the bee-like drone
of a Norelco. I polish the roughness
that pricks my palm, finding
a dimly glaring image, a moment not many
years ago, when a gentle, loving man calmly rose
from his chair, stood stiffly on his legs
and spoke my name, and I knew
his stone-like look meant *I am the father*.

John Warner Smith

ALCHEMY

My grandpa André didn't grow flowers,
only food, painlessly,
so I thought those mornings,
when I didn't see him waking, turning
dew-glazed grass and dirt, day after day
watching that black, bare ground
and the seeds he couldn't see.
With crickets sounding an alarm,
fire searing the clouds,
I thought of him while tip-toeing
across the lawn, balancing
two bowls of beer in my hands
to put inside the sweet potato vines
and trap leaf-eating snails.
By morning, I had fought earth,
flipped-flopped and bare-knuckled,
and conquered the wild,
untamable threat to man's dominion,
the old fashion way,
with alchemy for life after death,
like a young man who, long ago,
served time in state penitentiary,
went home and made a family,
grew melons sweet as cane syrup,
and sprayed WD-40 to loosen the joints
of his old, stiffening arthritic hands.

MENTOR

for Erb Fontenot

When the fires and lanterns had gone out
and he learned that three of us,
all Tenderfoots, had been heard talking
about girls in a nasty sort of way,
he entered our tent, scolded us,
and gave a lesson on how babies are made.

When we couldn't get to scout meetings,
because we lived ten miles away,
he bought the "Tin Can," an old school bus
that drove as badly as it looked,
but the radio worked just fine.

When we competed in our first swim meet,
he recruited three lifeguards
from the city pool across the river
to join our troop. We took the top ribbons
but never saw those boys again.

When we needed a theme for the jamboree,
he made us become "Scouts Around the World,"
dressed like photographs
we had cut out of *National Geographic*.
Again, we took the ribbons home.

When we needed an entry for the cake-off,
he had the school cooks to bake
a globe-cake three feet high. We frosted it
with shapes of all the continents, oceans
and seas, and took the top trophy.

When we got the invitation to march
in our first parade, he made us rehearse
for days. Singing patriotic songs, our strides
in perfect step, we stood tall as giants
as we passed the waving crowds.

When another troop at summer camp
instigated a fight and ganged up
on two of our scouts,
he planned a pre-dawn raid
on the troop's campsite.
Quieter than crickets, we crept
through black fog, deep
into the electric woods
and lay in the tall grass.
When he gave the command,
we charged, running like hyenas,
knocking down every tent pitched.

When a scout broke a rule,
he made him run the belt line,
a tunnel of hard-hitting licks,
fifty boys to a side.
Sixth-graders got double—his fan belt,
every lash on the palm
like the sting of a thousand bees.
Some boys jerked and jitterbugged.
Others stood proudly, like statues,
but he didn't stop swinging
until he saw tears.

When he got really angry with us,
the blood vessels in his temples swelled
and his lower jaw twitched.
We could feel his teeth gritting,
but he spoke with his eyes.

When our fathers weren't there, he was.

MAN

HIGHER GROUND

There was never enough water
for those hot summer days

when I was all flesh and feeling—acne,
shyness, a tweety bird voice,

lumps in my nipples
that looked like little breasts.

I gladly did the indoor chores, but
pinning her sheets, bras and panties

to a clothesline in the bare light
of day had become far too girly

for the boy who had grown
to hate the face that he feared

the world had been watching. I
needed freedom and space.

Maybe that's what I was feeling
when I told Mama, *I ain't doing that*

no more. I'm a man now.
She knew the storm had arrived,

a war had been declared,
but it took me years to realize

I was drowning and burning,
she was standing on higher ground.

John Warner Smith

First Love

> *You know you done me wrong baby*
> *And you'll be sorry someday*
> > —B. B. King, "The Thrill is Gone"

Maybe it was just coincidence, maybe
bad timing, but it seemed
when my first girlfriend and I broke up
all the hit R&B songs I'd hear
on Soul Hour were about heartbreak.
Aretha plainly asked

> *Don't play that song for me*
> *Cause it brings back memories*

but the DJs played it anyway,
until the words waxed inside my ears,

and I had sad tunes of my own, songs
without names, spinning inside my head
as I strolled down empty streets, alone
or with other boys of the night,
or when I drove to places
my ex-girl and I had been together,
thinking she might be there.

Gosh,

> *I was only seventeen*
> *I never dreamed she'd be so mean*

I couldn't see it then,

what had lived and died in the clouds

that last year in high school,
the smile in her eyes,
what she gave when her hand touched mine,
what she took when she stopped taking
my calls and wouldn't come to the door,

a blindness
I had wished could not feel
the pain of having been liked
so much by a girl
that I would call it love, then hate.

John Warner Smith

BAPTISM

One Sunday night we swayed
in a holy wind, wearing *Super Fly*
shirts and Eleganza shoes
we had seen at the Palace Theatre.
Life reeled in front of milk-crate squats,
between reefers and the poison
we gulped out of cheap port wine
mixed with fruit juice and spit.
Hitched a ride with a Viet Nam vet
turned hustler, whose Brougham,
half-primed, half-painted, choked
like a bleeding hog, blasting funk
from a plywood, shag-covered box:
Curtis, Santana, and our favorites—
soft horns and violins, high tenors
telling of broken-hearted men
and love we dreamt of making.
Peach-fuzzed and celluloid,
we cruised over Cyclops' bridge,
crept alleyways that stunk of piss,
and stood at a slut's bedside.
Would-be-gangbangers, candles
flickering on a frosted cake, we circled
her nakedness like a prayer vigil—
Awestruck. Eyes bulging. Legs
buckling on a thin sheet of lake ice.

JAKE'S ALLEY

Chad Harvey had enough of *that nigger*
taunting his girl. Spike Jones didn't
see the punch coming, but not even
Spike's cracked jaw could quell passion
flaring beneath the breezeways and oaks
where, almost in prayer, we recessed,
holding handbreadths of belief
in the sparkling faux of gemstones,
like the ones we saw on the bus ride
home after losing big to Byrd High.
Eyes on the back row seats flickered
like fireflies. Silly talk sifted glitter
out of granite until Bobby Miller said
I bet all girls are the same,
and on the spot I made up Cocoa Johnson:
pearly, black, and nasty enough
for rich white boys to risk a few bucks
for a quick creep across the color line.
Next day, in a pool room at Jake's Alley,
I went on a roll, breaking five straight
racks of nine ball, willing to bet it all
to have Lizzie Angelle, the tall blonde
who sat in homeroom. Miniskirt. Thighs
so gaped they spun any black boy's head
quicker than Chad's right hook.
But I knew the ghost of Jim Crow
would tiptoe before the sun went down.

John Warner Smith

SANDLOT

for Michael "Ashy Mo" Williams

I lost my only photograph of Ashy Mo
and me, reunited after thirty years,
standing inside Jones' Liquor Store
reminiscing about our glorious days
on Legion Street field, time
Ashy slipped around Big June's hold,
one-handed a button-hook
and took the pigskin
ninety-five yards for the score.

Like wildfire, game time
had spread house to house,
table to table, pool hall
to store-side crates,
every name called who came to play—
Van, Terry, Phillip, Edgar, Elray,
Andrew, all the Walls' and Guillory's,
even Charles: tongue tied
in a square knot, too slow for school,
his twisted, pigeon-toed
feet shuffling with the rhythm
of a white house party.

We huddled past twilight
inside imaginary bounds
of being gods and becoming men.
Who could forget
that icy-cold Strawberry Hill
night after a game, Ashy
and I kicking our shoes curbside
to settle the question

of who ran the fastest?

Lou Gehrig,
I suppose the photo is now of you
and him. I wonder
whether in Ashy's last days
he walked with a cane
or someone wheeled him
around or he lay stilled
by the breaths of his hardest run.

John Warner Smith

MEMORY BOARD

In heartache, she will feel
no affliction more painful
than sorrow hardened
by promises you failed to keep,
by her loneliness cried, trusting
kind words you tried to say
that brought no conciliation
and joy, only more sorrow.
She will think happiness,
a time when your laughter
was the sun and she felt
the weight of her troubles
melting as she watched you
calm the ripples of pebbles
skipping across a bay shore.
She'll remember warmth
that stirred the bird songs,
when you blushed
then browned and tore away,
falling inside a cold winter rain.
Years will pass, but she will
never forget your hurting words.

Deep Wound

Blood had not made its way

to the razor sting of the lash.
Something sweet and lush

about the white fat
below a deep layer of muscle,

the green weed and burrs
where the wound gaped like a ravine
before the dam of red water broke.

Something sweet and lush
about the halves of my leg
dangling on a thread of skin and bone,

and the pain that knotted inside,

needing to explode,
needing me to be manly.

John Warner Smith

Moving Men

Men of the moving company arrive
in gray crew neck shirts and hard-toe boots,
carrying dollies, ropes and quilts,
a few songs and small talk
to pass the time. They lift, pull
and raise, then sail the séance
of grit golden sands.
They pull cups, pour water,
and pass bread, potatoes and fried meat.
These cocoa tinted, bred, burned,
branded and bull-whipped men
have barely begun to move.
It's only morning. Give them a day.

Mrs. Taylor's Lunch Table

Morning pulled like taffy
those days we gathered at her table,
each minute a string strummed
pentatonic, every step hurried
onto the splintering pine boards
of her wooden front porch.
A bow unfettered hummed woodwinds
high above blue-belled gladiolas
blooming a chorus welcome.
Was it through wire mesh
tinted with faces smoked giddy
as flies flitting like jumping beans
that the scent of garlic and pork fat oozed?
Or was it rosewater, a brook
of old love and whiskered sweetness
wet as her kiss and checkered dress,
wrinkled, dripping kitchen sweat?

Clank and clatter of cast iron
and stained steel tuned sizzle,
crackling like sparks of amber
leaping a blacksmith's copper.
Feet wading, elbows touching leaf,
we gripped mahogany oars
while her memories swept ashore,
framed atop a cupboard
covered with embroidered lace.
Spoons stirred in the temple,
mounds of baked and fried meat,
yams, greens and a gumbo roux
that snapped the cold we brought
inside. We ate, laughed and talked

our way to Timbuktu,
wrapped in a healing linen heart,
oblivious to its gift and grace.

CHILD

REBIRTH

When I was fourteen,
I went searching for paramecium
and its predator, didinium.
Alone inside the water hyacinth,
dipping my Mason jar
into the pond, I heard
Careful, don't fall in,
as a hand behind me
cupped my crotch.
Like a mosquito hawk,
I darted deep into the air
until I could feel
the drum in my heart
and look back to see him—
his white mane palomino,
his cocked chapeau,
the mannequin-like grin
of a classmate's father.
I never told Mama and Daddy
how I became endowed
with the cheetah's speed,
the stealth and cunning
of a big catch that got away,
how life inside black water
had been fed and eaten, and
something inside me had died.

TREE POEM

for Jeremiah

I.

Your father died a month short of your third year,
four months after Hurricane Katrina.
Driving to Hattiesburg for his funeral, I watched
the flat land roll softly into the hills.
All the pines lay stiffly on the ground.

That morning, in the vestibule behind the sanctuary,
I sat with you and your brothers, waiting.
Jeremiah, stop running, I repeated.
Stop pushing, Jeremiah.
Joseph, leave him alone.
When they closed the casket, we went inside
to sit with the family.
No one wanted to cry aloud,
the air eerie as the eye of a storm.

II.

One hot summer day when you were five,
we drove to the mall. I know Autumn felt left out,
but I wanted to go shopping with only the boys.
The boulevard of the main entrance was old,
but the tall palm trees had just been planted.
Even I felt in a different place, wondering
why the branches still stood tied.

You sat in the back seat between Joseph and James,
while John Elisha sat up front.
Who has been here before? I asked,
to which you answered, *Not me, Paw Paw.*

48

When we shopped, you didn't want the same color
as Joseph's, so you picked green plaid short pants
with lines that clashed with the abstract design
of your pale green shirt. It said nothing
and everything about you.

III.

Jeremiah, you *had* been to the mall before,
with your brothers and me,
three days before your father's funeral.
The palm trees hadn't been planted yet.
But it was Christmastime.
Wreaths and red ribbons decked the boulevard,
and you saw Santa and bright-colored lights.
Like a butterfly fluttering on a blossoming bough,
you perched atop the carousel horse,
then flitted through the aisles of the toy store.

I know you don't remember. In time you may
hurt, even without the memory of your father.
Will you know his goodness and understand
why he took his life? Will you forgive him?
Will you stand tall in all seasons,
your branches blooming strong and wide?

When we left the mall, we went to the Mississippi River
and stood on the levee to watch barges
drag the current. Like logs, we rolled our bodies
down the steep slope, our arms raised high,
giving ourselves to the ground and open air.

John Warner Smith

AN ARTIST REFLECTS ON HIS CREATIONS
for Xzavion (2004–2012)

I don't name the ones outside
my mirrors, left to drift,
knocking on my doors,
peeking through papery walls

and wooden beams, shuttered
from my memory
to their dying breaths,
the ones I bruise

who break and fall then rise
from the blackened abyss
wearing faces my shadow sheds
to stalk my bedlam dreams,

the ones smitten by light,
who grow to bloom
nobly and picturesque,
sparkling in the city squares,

praying in a thousand tongues
that shatter the cathedral glass.
I name the brown ones,
color them alabaster

to make a pond
reflect a leafy canopy
in a *Sunday Picnic* painting
that can't color pain

of a child in the tree house.
I call him Xzavion,
blood of my blood,
flesh of my flesh,

living inside my mirrors,
doors and tearing walls,
my hammering hands
writing a dark song of rage.

John Warner Smith

VILLANELLE TO BOY X

when you hide the pains you hold beneath a dark starless sky

can they become memories told   will tender brighter days unfold

the past you know will always lie   when you hide the pains you hold

and shutter secrets in the cold   if shattered dreams never die

can they become memories told   what blank torn pages you fold

on starry nights that pass you by   when you hide the pains you hold

truths more precious than gold   heal the hurt your soul will cry

can they become memories told   when you grow strong and old

enough to know the reason why   when you hide the pains you hold

           can they become memories told

WORLD CHILD

Any child in any country will fall
from a toy, onto the ground. He will
pause, and the silence will seem forever,
but you know what follows,
that long bellowing cry
the one that stirs ants
and makes the starlings fly away.
Eventually, the child lets the cry go
and the whole world takes notice,
but you don't see blood or a cut,
not even a scratch. You touch
the child's bruise, kiss it
and tell him he will be alright,
that the bruise is only a bobo
or something like that,
and the moment you touch the child
and speak, his tears stop,
and he stands up and begins
to do the playful things children do.
Such a child, whose nightmares
of violence and death might never
wake, never knows when or how
evil stalks. Like a windblown wildfire
in midday sun, abuse, famine
or disease strikes. Innocence
is scourged. Humanity knells defeat.

DIXIE

No named street, no yards
or playground to call our own,
only small plots of dirt between sidewalks
laid like crosses or grave markers
for names of large families
who lived in the sprawling red duplexes
the government had built.

I didn't know the meaning of Dixie
until I read American history,
but no one ever said
the projects and *across the track*s meant
colored and poor. No one taught that
Dixie meant hate.

Some words we spoke
I never saw in print, like *cush cush*,
which meant dinner when there was little
else to eat except yellow corn meal
mixed with salt and water, then
cooked in a black iron skillet
until fluffed and nearly burnt,
served with milk and figs.

Birth and death came early but naturally.
Never a siren or flashing light.
And we didn't have seasons, just days
spent catching sunbeams, hopping tombs
or making games out of rocks and sticks.

Neighbors didn't lock their doors.
We entered without knocking

or peeped inside, pressing our noses
against the busted, smoke-black screens,
sniffing baked bread, fried fish,
and scents of drudgery.
Like family, we ate.

A half-century later, families gone,
doors and windows boarded,
the buildings still stand.
So does the name.

John Warner Smith

BABY AND THE BELL RINGERS

Brother said the first time I swallowed
Mama's breast milk, I threw up.
She slapped me and cursed, then
dropped me to the floor, left me
alone under an open window,
where bugs bit my arms and legs.
Sister said I looked like a balloon.

I never learned how to say words
but I know sounds. I can giggle
and cry, and I like to play
pattycake and beat a drum.
I don't remember anything
outside the room where we live,
except for one night a long time ago,
when Mama put me in a blanket
and showed me the sky.
Some of the lights came down
and put their hands out
to touch me, but she pulled me
away. Every night since then,
when I close my eyes to sleep,
they come back, and I hear them
playing a song, like bells.

Everybody calls me *Baby*,
but nobody feeds me anymore,
and they don't clean me
when I mess on myself. Bugs crawl
all over me, and my sores bleed
and hurt when I scratch.
I don't know how old I am

or what my face looks like.
I think I am tall, almost a man,
but my legs can't hold up my body,
so I lie here all day, waiting
for nighttime and the bells to come.

HERO

CHURINGA

When he died, a photograph haunted me
like a buried rock. My hands, a sieve,
sifted time and memory, parted flesh
from dry bones and bitter earth

until I found no photograph of me
standing beside Nelson Mandela,
not close enough for his hand to touch
mine before the bodyguard would say

no more handshakes, back away,
and a sterner voice would yell
please, no flash, they harm
the president's eyes. I remember

those eyes, how they danced
the toyi toyi and told a griot's tale
of freedom warriors beating spears
into pruning hooks. I had watched

him stand stilted as a soldier.
Like paisley on his primly fitting shirt,
the aura of his boyish bloom
camouflaging pomp and panache.

Spellbound by mana, it was I
who had aimed the camera's lens,
creating my churinga, numinous
as the cloak and crown not worn

by a king who had come down
to the valley, walked the dirt floors

of our village, slept in a shanty hut
and eaten our small pot food.

Soul Be A Witness

I: Day One

[District Attorney Percy Ogden]

Gentlemen of the jury,
Emile Hebert has confessed to killing
Austin P. Landry of Acadia Parish.
He also admitted firing the shot
that seriously injured Jules Broussard of Youngsville,
that same shot that hit our honorable Sheriff
and may well have rendered him partially
incapable of fulfilling his lawful duty.

We have spent a day and a half selecting
you twelve fair-minded men,
whom we pray will bring justice
to this tragedy and horror.
As witness will swear, Emile Hebert,
one trained in the use of firearms,
pointed a single-barrel shotgun
toward Austin P. Landry at short range,
pulled the trigger without warning
and hit the victim below the heart.
As the Sheriff shot, Hebert fired again
with intent to kill the entire party in distress,
including Broussard's younger brother
and Julius Delahoussaye, a race jockey
of the Fair Grounds track,
both of whom escaped unharmed.

Hebert's defense will say he was provoked.
But gentlemen I say to you,

provocation of anger is only an excuse;
it cannot under any circumstances
justify these crimes.
This is not a question
of Hebert's guilt or innocence.
It is a test of your moral courage
to rightly conclude
that Emile Hebert should be
lawfully hooded, noosed and dropped
from the public gallows
at a crystal blue high noon
for the murder and mass assault
he has committed.

[Sheriff Felix Latiolas]

Mes bons amis, I am grateful to be alive to speak
this truth. It was a horrifying night.
When the car stalled, we walked to the refinery
and secured help of the Broussard brothers.
We found a spade to help with the mud.
On the way back to the car, we met Hebert
in the buggy. He demanded the right of way,
so we moved to one side to let him pass.
We asked Hebert to stop and help with the car.
He yelled and cursed, then he raised his barrel
and pumped a shot into young Austin Landry.
In one motion, I slung the spade at the buggy
and pulled my revolver. The spade struck
Hebert's wife, who tipped over with the baby.
I barely let go a shot before Hebert fired again,

hitting Jules Broussard and me. I tell you,
Emile's rage was like a bonfire, but not surprising.
On many occasion I was summoned to fights
at the colored gambling shack on Verot,
oftentimes involving Emile and his brothers,
not to mention times they disrespected
good upstanding white people of this parish.
City Marshal Stutes was smart to arrest John Hebert,
brother of Emile, on the night of the killing,
knowing John's quick temper.

[Julius Delahoussaye]

I was lucky to escape without injury
when Hebert fired the shots.
It happened the way the Sheriff said.
Emile was in a fit of rage.
The boom of his blasts rattled my ears.
Pellets spattered like hail,
pelting flesh and bone.
The air was smoke and powder
and men groaning.
The Sheriff showed courage
in pulling his revolver,
but it was no match
for the 12-gauge pump
raining down from the buggy.

[City Marshal Stutes of Youngsville]

We were a posse of twelve riding four to a car.
    Some had already gone to arrest John Hebert
        as precaution against more violence.

We arrived at Emile's residence
    near 5 o'clock in the morning
        and found him coming out of the barn.

The wife was asleep in the house.
    I don't know which was calmer,
        Hebert or the dead winds

of the storm that passed.
    His silence spooked me.
        The horse and buggy had been cleaned,

muddy clothes soaked in the trough,
    and the gun was not to be found.
        Hebert surrendered without resistance.

Upon arrival at the jail,
    he confessed to the shooting
        and to tossing the weapon in a field.

[Emile Hebert]

Sir, as my soul is a witness, I meant no harm.
We had gone to visit my daddy near Youngsville.
Near midnight, we had no stars or moon.

The rain had been heavy. Mud was boot-high
and the buggy barely rolled. My horse pushed back
on the crack of the whip. Not far from the mill
we met men walking, Sheriff Felix,
with a race jockey and others. They said
the car had stalled and told me to release
the buggy. When I refused, they threatened
to take it, so I raised the barrel of my gun.
One of the men threw an iron,
causing Leona and the baby to fall.
The horse bucked and the wheel rolled
with them below. I pumped my barrel
not seeing where the buckshot fell.
The Sheriff fired his handgun and missed,
but my second round hit him
before he could shoot again.
Two other men went down.
Two of them fled.

[Defense Attorney John L. Kennedy]

Honorable men of the jury,
earlier you heard testimony of the State's
witnesses, that which clearly conflicts
with testimony of the defendant.

You have seen this man's remorse
and heard him say
that his heart felt no malice
toward the men he encountered.

He aimed his gun to give warning,
but he shot, as any man would,
to defend himself, his wife,
and child barely three months old.

Even now he fears for his life.
As you know, Your Honor, shortly after
Emile and his wife Leona were arrested,
vigilantes plotted to overtake the jail.

In your wisdom you moved Emile
forty miles to the Franklin jail,
and you were wise to deploy
sixty National Guardsmen

to pitch tents on these grounds,
it being rumored that five hundred men
from Acadia Parish would try
again to take the prisoner.

For two days and nights,
in heavy downpour,
the guardsmen have stood watch.
Even now they stand armed

at our doors as mobs gather
with hate and vengeance
in their eyes. It is a wonder
we have a trial and a jury.

II: Day Two

[Charley Harrison]

Yes, sir, I have known Emile all my life.
  We went to the war together and came home.

We now work the fields for Mr. Voorhies.
  Sir, I do remember that night.

It was Tuesday, past midnight, late June.
  I was sleeping and heard loud sound

like drums beating.
  Emile was standing at the porch screen

covered in mud. He had Leona and the baby.
  Emile told me how he met the men

walking on the road, Sheriff Felix and others.
  He said the men told him to move the buggy

and help them push the car from the mud.
  He said they threatened to take him down

so he raised his shotgun to warn.
  He said one of the men threw an iron

and knocked Leona and the baby to the road.
  He said he shot, then the Sheriff shot,

then he shot again and the Sheriff fell.

He said two other men were down.

Emile told me he threw the gun in the field
  a mile back, where the road forked.

At sunup I went to the field and fetched the gun.
  When deputies came and asked me

if I had seen Emile that night, I told them
  all I knew and all that Emile said,

and I gave them the gun I had fetched.
  That is all I know, sir.

[Victor Hebert]

Of my nine sons, Emile
speaks his mind,
but he would never shoot a man
unless he had to.
He and John went to the Great War.
He killed men then.
In the hunt he is always the best shot,
but he would never shoot a man
unless he had to.
You know my family
as you know your own.
For some of you
we built the fields and crop.
Emile and Leona had come to visit.
The storm kept them late.

They wanted to get home.
They didn't want trouble.
When deputies came to see me,
I left barefoot, afraid
the hangmen would soon find him.
Emile would not hurt any man
unless he had to.

[Defense Attorney Sidney Roos]

Distinguished jurymen,
surely it is too much to ask of you
to not see Emile Hebert as a colored man,
one of Creole descent, defiant in some ways,
one who never tips his hat.

But it is not much to ask
that you see Emile as a man
who just four years ago
fought side by side
with your own sons and brothers
face down in the dirt trenches
and green fields of France
to protect our freedom and democracy,
a decorated soldier
of the all-colored infantry.

Good men of this jury,
this is 1922, not yet winter.
Already forty Negroes
have been unlawfully hung

in our beloved nation.
At least five men, colored and white,
have been reported lynched in Louisiana.
Some have vanished in broad daylight
never to be seen again.

Just a month ago, five men in Mer Rouge
were kidnapped and are still not found.
One of them, F. W. Daniels, fought bravely
in the Great War as did our defendant.
Many urge our own Governor John M. Parker
to call on President Harding to intercede
and stop the rampage of the invisible empire
that terrorizes and spills innocent blood
across the sweet soils of our state.

I beg you, gentlemen,
in the name of honor and decency,
do not stain these august, pristine halls
with the same blood of injustice.
Declare this man innocent,
set him free
and return him to his wife and child.

[District Attorney Percy Ogden]

As surely as my duty
is to prosecute violators of the law,
I support Judge Campbell's action
to ensure safety of the prisoner,
including his decision to keep the peace

by bringing militia into this courtyard
for the first time in parish history,
and searching those who enter.
I, too, would urge our Governor
to stop the rampant violent acts of the KKK
by whatever means possible.
The tyranny must cease.
But let us be clear.
Whether he be Negro or Caucasian,
and with due respect to the honorable service
he has given our country,
Emile Hebert is a confessed murderer.
It is he who is on trial here,
not the Ku Klux Klan.
It is he who terrorized
and caused innocent blood to be spilled,
namely the blood of Austin P. Landry
that spewed from his arteries
into the black mud of a cane field.
And what about the deceased
victim's wife and children,
awakened from their night dreams
to find a nightmare come true?

Gentlemen, having heard the true account
of what happened that night,
as spoken by Sheriff Felix Latiolais
and by Julius Delahoussaye,
both being eyewitness to the shooting,
you now have a duty
to rise and render judgment,
judgment Hebert justly deserves,

that being the verdict of guilty—
guilty of murder and mass assault
of the first degree.
I pray you Godspeed.

III: The Verdict

[Jury Foreman L.P. DeBlanc]

Yesterday we were taken to our quarters
shortly after sundown. The night was long
and sleepless. We are now left to conclude
that our collective sense cannot distinguish
between twilight and night. There is law
and there is justice. We find it impossible
to reconcile them. Final judgment might
best be left to means beyond our reason.
We leave that to the interpreters of law
to decide. We are farmers, storekeepers
and laborers of industry, some learned,
some not, but all cherish the sovereignty
of property and the comfort of order.
I believe I speak for every juryman here.
None condones violence or the violation
of rights, be they property or human.
But neither can we condone abuse
of power or the partial execution of law.
What happened that horrifying night
on Sugar Mill Road was a duel, not
of firearms, but of principles. Of what

has been spoken during this trial, we
can discern neither truth nor falsehood.

[District Judge William Campbell]

Well, a surprising verdict indeed, but then,
not so surprising in light of the case
that has been presented and the testimony
we have heard these past two days.

Having heard the jury foreman's most eloquent
statement, I hereby declare this a mistrial.
Thank you, gentlemen, for your service.
I am also indebted to our National Guardsmen.

This case is now remanded back to the State
to decide whether it will retry the accused.
In the meantime, the prisoner shall remain
shackled and in custody, pending bail.

Note:

Twenty-six-year-old Emile Hebert was never retried. Transcriptions of court records
of the testimonies do not exist. The dialog portrayed here is conjectured, based
largely upon newspaper reports of the case. In November 1922, Governor John
M. Parker of Louisiana went to Washington, D.C., to ask President Harding and
the Federal Bureau of Investigation to help end the KKK violence in that state. A
month later, two of the five kidnapped men of Mer Rouge were found in a lake.
Their bodies had been mutilated. One of the bodies was that of F. W. Daniels.
Condemnation of the Ku Klux Klan became a personal crusade of Governor Parker
and a hallmark of his administration.

SELF

You

I once read a tale of a carpenter
who saw an oak and said to it:
You are useless because you are old,
you never bear fruit,
and your wood could never be used
to build anything. That evening,
as the carpenter slept, the oak appeared
to him in a dream. *Why,* the oak asked,
do you compare me to trees
that are pilfered and broken
and die young? You poor mortal,
would I have become so old and great
if I had been useful in any way?

There comes a time in your journey
when gray clouds begin to gather.
The view ahead grows hazy, then dark,
but the road is familiar, marked,
and filled with a world of travelers.
You feel an urge to turn,
take a different path, abandon
the known and let go of the ground below.
But you doubt and fear, not knowing
where the path will take you, why it tugs
like a rock in your gut, so you stay
the familiar course, hoping it fulfills
your needs or leads to some purpose.
Again and again you feel the road
bending inside you. Still, you resist
the turn. Restless, confused,
but assured by the company of others,
you look back and straight ahead.

79

Finally, on the darkest night, you yield
to the haunting whisper that only you
can hear, and you turn, alone.
Soon, the path is a whirling sea,
filled with peril. You stumble, fall,
feel lost, hurt and betrayed by faith.
Still, you press on into the blindness
and shivering sounds of night. Ignoring
the trumpeting voices, the hands
that pull and hold, you press on,
falling and getting up, doubting
and believing, until one day, decades
later perhaps, the window of heaven opens
and a person inside you appears—a man
with more strength and peace
than you could have dreamt or imagined.
You had lived to be your great purpose.

THE OTHER

I.

Alone on the porch in the black drip
of evening. Branches of a Bradford pear
bend in the riff of sleet lashing
winter's bareness, drowning the crackle
of leaves that touch and tear away.
In the eaves, something small, brown
and feathery rests, still
or lifeless, like broken bark
or twigs of a bird's nest
tossed by the whirling wind.
I think of house wakes long ago,
their greetings and smiles,
ephemeral as flowers, cradling death.

II.

A blank memory, that face—
the fair-skinned man who drove
Grandmother Rose and me through a storm
to see her father lying in a coffin
high above a wooden floor.
I sit beside a window, a slingshot
hit from the pears dropping.
The men inside circle each other,
talking, eating and drinking,
while women kneel and pray
with beads dangling in their hands.
Mama, for weeks a dim fading light,
shining for a moment, then,
like the bird puddle, gone again.

John Warner Smith

Ten years later, I am fourteen,
alone, strolling toward a sun setting.
I enter a crowded living room
where my best friend's mother lies
under a raised, satin-lined lid
like a broken bough
fallen into a bed of orchids.
He lifts her pink veil and gestures.
I lean forward, shut my eyes
and press my lips to hers,
not fearing she will move.
Hours later, as I walk hurriedly
into the blue-black night,
her pallid, stone-like face appears
in the bone-white moon.

III.

The icy stillness of dead wood
pulls me closer. Suddenly,
a thimble head and beak twitch,
then slowly turn toward me.
I step onto the ground,
blossoms dormant deep below—
orchids that will rise in springtime
and tangle wildly in a honeysuckle vine,
making a sweet love scent
that stirs the calm morning air,
like the first whir of newborn wings
that snap and dart into the world.

Rebuilding

The city's blood had been her air,
her sounds and smells in crowded squares,
a murky river asleep beside her.
The storm made her breathless.
When the sun died and was reborn
we were not there, only the brown pelicans.
Spreading their candelabrum wings,
the pelicans raised their giant jaws
and began the long journey home.
Deep in the marsh, miles away
from the unraveling sky, mangrove roots
lay torn and twisted, branches tossed.
Twig by twig the mandibles and bills
wove their cross-stitches
and rebuilt their breeding nests.

John Warner Smith

HELLO AND WELCOME, ONCE AGAIN, TO NINETY SECONDS OF *KEEPING IT REAL*

This is Reverend Reggie "RB" Bennett
of New Refuge Temple, speaking live
on WXOQ–AM, broadcasting
from Ron's Barber Shop on Claiborne.
Another anniversary of Katrina,
and residents of the Lower Nine stand
in scorching, Sahara-like heat,
protesting the snail pace of rebuilding
what they used to call a community.
Amen? Now a wasteland of weeds.
They stand at the foot of a levee
that made a tomb of their dreams,
washed out like a pit of dead bones.
Let's be real. The government failed.
Everyone knows it. Amen? Broke us
like scattered pieces of fallen crystal,
put our jazz in the belly of a whale,
and left us singing the blues—what
the government didn't do, still ain't
doing. Amen? An American tragedy,
another chapter in a long sorry tale
of *them that got and them that gets*,
old as money and slavery. As always,
strength be with you in the struggle,
but as Fats would say, *I've got no time
for talkin'. I've got to keep on walkin'.*

BIRD NESTS

One Sunday, while lavender bloomed
high above the garden, I visited an old aunt
in Room 60, her new home. Like bird nests,
her lifelong belongings had been tossed to the floor.

From one of the two bundles, I lifted
a blue hooded shirt and pulled it over her head
and shoulders. I slipped a pair of wool clogs
on her feet, then lifted her arms to a walker.

The scars of madness had faded in her face,
shrunken now with thick manly brows, her body
frail as a broken-winged sparrow, weightless
in the air she struggled to breathe, in the pain

she could not speak of. I imagine she slept
the way I saw her the following Friday,
lying on her back, mouth open and gasping,
her forehead cool as spring water, hair soft

as hand-sewn silk. After the cup-shaped petals
had fallen, I would see her once more. Again,
I gathered the straws of her wind-torn nests,
one of them still bundled, strewn to the floor.

John Warner Smith

FENCES

Not much has changed since days long ago,
when the only things that separated
my parents' front yard from white families
were a boulevard, a field of tall grass
and the walls of Jim Crow segregation,
except at the neighborhood grocery store,
where everybody's money was welcome.
I have my own back yard now,
and white neighbors all around,
enclosed by fences they built
after I moved in. We politely greet
with first names. We shop the bargains
and root for the local sports teams.
From my back porch, I often sit
and listen to them playing soul music.
But we pray in separate churches,
send our kids to separate schools,
and vote for different political parties.
Sometimes, I feel just one song, one
prayer, one raging shout away
from tearing the walls and fences down.

PARTED

When I was ten years old my stepfather fished
a sparkling new Schwinn bicycle out of the coulee
bordering our back yard. All the boys knew
it had been found. Still, I was the envy of the world,
Bellerophon sailing in the wing breaths of Pegasus,
on my way to conquer Chimera. I named her Silver Bell,
my first girl—all curves and chrome—her frame,
wheels, fenders, headlight and front spring.
I'd spend hours polishing her with 3-In-One oil
and steel wool, tightening every bolt and spoke
with wrenches borrowed from my father's toolbox.

And then, one July Sunday morning, decades after
I had become a man, Daddy died. Both parents now
gone, I was alone, not knowing what I didn't know
and couldn't feel, masking a world broken by grief.
Some nights I only heard howling winds, improvisations
without refrains, boughs bending roughly in the riffs.
Untying tangled threads of blood in a newborn heart,
I caught hold of wings destined for nowhere.
I didn't think about my dying with their deaths until,
finally, I boxed the last keepsake and buried
a part of me inside the rusted toolbox I left behind.

SPIRIT

1.

The older I grow, the more I want to see
God, lie down with Him
beside a stream in a green pasture
stretching beyond the reach of my eyes.

Is it lustful to yearn for a mouth
and hand to taste and touch my flesh,
or is it the archetypal fantasia,
an ancient hunger buried inside me
long before the birth water broke?

Merciful daemon, are you the familiar
yet strange scent that fills the air
when a sudden burst of rain
is not enough to settle the whirling dust?
When you come again, when you go
into the sky, take my shadow with you.

2.

When my father began to lose his mind,
he would point to say which direction
I should turn the car. I knew the way,
and his pointing agitated me.
In time, his memory of me shattered.
When his mind became a desert,
I had him committed, a foreign country
to him, locked inside a tall iron fence.

One night, miles away, my car screeching
toward a head-on crash, I closed my eyes

to brace for impact. Suddenly, I felt
the motion of a hand other than mine,
the car careening, spinning into the abyss,
until the blunt, broadside hit. I landed
inside a shallow ditch, barely injured.

3.
Sometimes, with our eyes open wide,
we find our way only by song.

We can name this creation, call it grace
or truth if words are what we need

to believe that we can live forever
or move mountains, if we haven't taken

more than we've given. Sometimes,
the sound enters us, takes hold,

makes us dance, cry, or die for love
or freedom, but we know this song

is fleeting. We cannot mold it, make it
our own, because no one can possess

such a free, perfect, beautiful thing,
and nothing can replicate the feeling

that it puts inside us. This *Not I*,
this *Other* lives only in a moment,

a gift: pure and whole, passing,
staying just long enough to be felt.

4.

When I was a young husband and father,
I lost a job that I had made great sacrifices
to get. Blind and broken-winged,
a bird with a dream that choked of faith.
We moved to another city,
where I took a job in a small cubicle
with no door, working to improve
the lives of poor people. Eventually,
I became the manager of that city,
but along the way, many doors
I had prayed would open stayed shut.

Now, the sun falling, ambition waned,
and my sight growing dim,
I merely watch who I once was,
who others saw and see. In the distance,
a foghorn howls, but I believe
there is light where I am going.
Maybe death will spare
the bitter cold ocean night.
Maybe I will feel the song
and dance on the white-capped waves.

A Road That Bends

On a road we travel
lies a graveyard
just beyond the willows
that creep to the edge
of the world and speak, slumping,
turning the road,
pulling us inside
wild, tangled roots.

Except to turn around
or tend the small plots,
few who drive by ever notice
sunken cement beds
behind the broken fence
draped by wild grass.

In a yard of bones
the dead live among themselves,
not keeping company
with souls yards away
who step hurriedly, desperate
in their pursuit of life.

The tombs, dark, forgotten,
sacred and cursed,
bend the road, calling us.

About the Author

JOHN WARNER SMITH's poems have appeared in *Ploughshares*, *Callaloo*, *Antioch Review*, *Transition*, *The Worcester Review*, and other literary journals. His debut poetry collection, *A Mandala of Hands*, was published by Aldrich Press / Kelsay Books in 2015. Smith's poems have been nominated for the Pushcart Prize and the Best of the Net Anthology. A Cave Canem Fellow, Smith earned his MFA in Creative Writing at the University of New Orleans. His poetry can be found at www.johnwarnersmith.com.